MTLE Earth and Space Science Exam

"You never fail until you stop trying" - Albert Einstein

For inquiries;
info@xmprep.com

MTLE Earth and Space Science Exam #1

Test Taking Tips

☐ Take a deep breath and relax

☐ Read directions carefully

☐ Read the questions thoroughly

☐ Make sure you understand what is being asked

☐ Go over all of the choices before you answer

☐ Paraphrase the question

☐ Eliminate the options you know are wrong

☐ Check your work

☐ Think positively and do your best

Table of Contents

TEST DIRECTION

DIRECTIONS

Read the questions carefully and then choose the ONE best answer to each question.

Be sure to allocate your time carefully so you are able to complete the entire test within the testing session. You may go back and review your answers at any time.

You may use any available space in your test booklet for scratch work.

Questions in this booklet are not actual test questions but they are the samples for commonly asked questions.

This test aims to cover all topics which may appear on the actual test. However some topics may not be covered.

Studying this booklet will be preparing you for the actual test. It will not guarantee improving your test score but it will help you pass your exam on the first attempt.

Some useful tips for answering multiple choice questions;

- Start with the questions that you can easily answer.

- Underline the keywords in the question.

- Be sure to read all the choices given.

- Watch for keywords such as NOT, always, only, all, never, completely.

- Do not forget to answer every question.

1

The moon is an astronomical body that orbits the Earth, making it the only permanent natural satellite the Earth has.

How much smaller is the moon as compared to the Earth?

A) The moon and the Earth are of the same size.

B) The moon is about one half the size of the Earth.

C) The moon is about one fourth the size of the Earth.

D) The moon is about one eighth the size of the Earth.

2

A psychrometer is an instrument that uses the difference in readings between two thermometers, one having a wet bulb and the other having a dry bulb. It measures the moisture content of the air.

Which principle does a psychrometer is based on?

A) By comparing the evaporative cooling that occurs in a particular location to the air temperature, the relative humidity can be calculated.

B) The apparent temperature can be identified by comparing the actual temperature in a location with the relative humidity.

C) By calculating the molecular weight of dry air to the molecular weight of the actual air, the density of an air mass can be determined.

D) By comparing the actual pressure in a location to the theoretical sea-level pressure, the adiabatic cooling of an air mass can be determined.

3

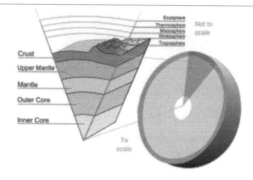

Which of the following can identify the structure of the Earth's core, mantle, and lower crust best?

A) Measuring the intensity and fluctuations of Earth's magnetic field

B) Examining the properties of lava

C) Collecting samples from deep boreholes drilled into Earth

D) Studying the speeds and travel paths of seismic waves passing through Earth

4

In astronomy, the most commonly used measures of distance are the light year, parsec and astronomical unit.

Which of the following is not a correct explanation?

A) A light-year is a distance that light can travel in one year in a vacuum (space).

B) One parsec is defined as the distance to a star that shifts by one arcsecond from one side of Earth's orbit to the other.

C) The astronomical unit (AU) is a unit of length, roughly the average distance from Earth to the Sun. Astronomical units are usually used to measure distances within our solar system.

D) Light years are usually used to measure distances within our solar system; Astronomical units are used to measure distances between the galaxies.

5

What causes the variations in tidal ranges across some localities?

A) The difference between the relative positions of the Moon and the Sun from the Earth

B) The Coriolis effect and rotation of the Earth on its axis

C) The ocean floor topography and the coastline shapes

D) The winds' direction

6

Which of the following protects Earth from harmful charged particles coming from outer space?

A) Earth's magnetic field

B) Chemical reaction from gases

C) Ozone layer

D) Density of atmosphere

7

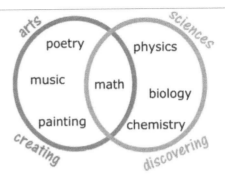

What is the primary reason why mathematics is assumed to be the language of science?

A) It has no cultural bias associated with its practice.

B) It describes predictable and testable relationships.

C) It reduces the uncertainty associated with chaotic systems.

D) It relies on the same processes as science.

8

Which of the following scientific skills do you use when you see that the sky is cloudy?

A) Making observation

B) Drawing conclusion

C) Making inference

D) Posing a question

9

What contributes most of the dissolved salts in the Earth's oceans?

A) The marine biological activities

B) The atmospheric deposition

C) The weathering of continental rocks

D) The eruptions of hotspot volcanoes under the oceans

10

How do lichens, plant roots, and fungi are able to weather rock chemically?

A) By drawing molecular water from the crystals that make up the rock

B) By producing acids that cause the decomposition of the rock

C) By extracting minerals directly from the rock through osmosis

D) By manufacturing salts that alter the rock's crystal structure

11

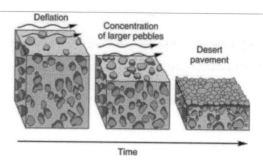

Desert pavement phenomenon happens when a thin layer of closely packed pebbles and cobbles covers the ground surface.

What is the primary cause of this phenomenon?

A) The differential erosion of sediments by wind

B) The slow dispersal of material from the base of alluvial fans by gravity

C) The breakup of bedrock under hot and dry conditions

D) The deposition of coarse-grained sediments during flash flooding

12

Fog is a cloudlike layer of water droplets or ice crystals near the surface of the earth which reduces the visibility.

When is an advection fog most likely to occur?

A) A layer of warmer air traps a cold air beneath it.

B) A hot dry air in the surface cools after sunset.

C) A cool moist air warms as it flows down a mountainside.

D) A warm moist air flows over cold ocean water.

13

A scientist collects and tests the pH of water from six local ponds following significant rainstorms to determine whether rainfall increases the acidity of pond water.

What is lacking in the scientist's experiment that is the most significant flaw in his experimental design?

A) Manipulated variables

B) A clear hypothesis

C) Control data

D) A dependent variable

14

Which statement below illustrates a scientific inference?

A) Based on the data, Mars once had liquid water.

B) Gathering repeated measurements will reduce random error.

C) Proper handling of electrical equipment involves putting a ground wire.

D) There are three significant figures in a certain measurement.

15

Geologists use the Bowen's reaction series to explain the occurrence of various minerals in a particular igneous rock.

Which of the following events does it primarily define?

A) Different minerals in magma have different solidification temperature.

B) Crystals grow within a cooling magma at a particular rate.

C) There are different chemical changes that occur after a rock has solidified.

D) There are various crystal systems that will develop as a rock forms under pressure.

Which of the following explains the presence of the Earth's core which is composed of iron and nickel?

A) The heavier elements are pulled toward the core by the intense gravitational field at the center of Earth.

B) Earth was originally formed as a solid which eventually melted, and the denser iron and nickel sank down through the less dense layers of silicate material to the center.

C) The ancient Earth was initially composed of iron and nickel, and the rest of the planet was added later by accretion.

D) The Earth's magnetic field pulls molten iron and nickel toward the center, leaving nonmagnetic silicates behind.

Minerals such as gold, platinum, and native copper are formed in concentrated placer deposits in alluvial sands and gravels.

Which of the following explains this formation?

A) These materials are formed because they are resistant to chemical weathering than the surrounding matrix.

B) These minerals are formed because they have smaller grains than most other minerals.

C) These minerals resist displacement by moving water.

D) These materials are deposited quickly when stream velocity decreases due to their higher gravity properties.

CONTINUE ▶

18

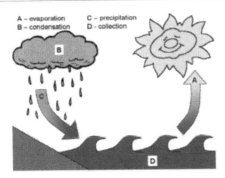

A – evaporation   C – precipitation
B – condensation   D - collection

When does the condensation in the atmosphere occur?

A) After a rapid increase in the concentration of water vapor in the clouds

B) When there are microscopic particles in the atmosphere

C) When the relative humidity is slightly over 100 percent

D) When there are significant contrasts in temperature across the regions

19

The winds at the Earth's surface typically flow across the isobars that separate a high-pressure center from a low-pressure center, while the wind flow aloft is typically parallel to atmospheric pressure isobars.

What is most likely causing the difference between wind flow aloft and at the Earth's surface?

A) The increased frictional drag on wind flow at the surface of the Earth

B) The reduced strength of the Coriolis effect on wind flow aloft

C) The greater divergence of winds above a low-pressure system

D) The decreased atmospheric pressure with increased altitude

Which of the following best helps to explain why some localities have normally great tidal ranges (up to 60 feet) and others have one- to two-foot tidal ranges?

A) The relative positions of the Moon and Sun are different at different localities.

B) The Coriolis effect and rotation of the Earth tend to enhance tidal bow in the higher latitudes.

C) Ocean floor topography and the shape of the coastline serve to amplify tidal bow at specific localities.

D) Tradewinds push the water into large tidal bulges near rocky shorelines.

Dr. Morris suspects that the data he is collecting from an experiment may have a random error.

Which of the following is the best thing that Dr. Morris can do?

A) Identify any factors that could have caused the error and repeat the experiment to check the consistency of the data.

B) Show the results of the study to his expert colleagues to check for careless errors.

C) Change the hypothesis and begin the experimental process again adhering to the steps of the scientific method.

D) Recalibrate the instrument used in data measurement and perform the experiment once more.

22

How do water vapor and carbon dioxide affect the radiation emitted by the Sun and Earth?

A) Carbon dioxide and water vapor absorb ultraviolet radiation emitted by the Sun, and they transmit it as an infrared radiation from Earth's surface into the upper atmosphere.

B) Carbon dioxide and water vapor absorb much of the ultraviolet radiation from the sun, and they transmit it as a visible light reflected from Earth's surface.

C) Carbon dioxide and water vapor absorb the infrared radiation released by the Sun, and they trap it as an ultraviolet radiation in the lower atmosphere of the Earth.

D) Carbon dioxide and water vapor allow much of the Sun's radiation to reach Earth's surface, but they absorb much of the infrared radiation emitted by Earth.

23

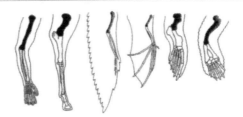

Which of the following reasons will most likely result in the similarity of design in the mammalian appendages shown above?

A) Common ancestry
B) Evolutionary convergence
C) Geographic isolation
D) Directional selection

A deep well which is a confined aquifer has been contaminated with petroleum. To investigate the source of the petroleum contaminant, test wells were drilled in the north, east, south, and west areas near the well. The samples were taken from the north and the east wells were found to be contaminated, while those from the south and the west wells were not.

It was concluded that the contaminant must be coming from the north and the east.

If the conclusion is not valid, which of the following can be the reason of it?

A) The samples were collected by different people.

B) The north and the east test wells are on the upgradient side of the original well where groundwater in the confined aquifer flows toward it.

C) The samples from the north and the south wells were collected when the well pump was off, while the other samples were collected when it was on.

D) The south and the west wells were drilled shallow above the confined aquifer.

The scientific method is a process for experimentation that is used to explore observations and answer questions.

Which of the following is the correct order of the steps in the scientific method?

A) Asking a question, making a hypothesis, testing the hypothesis, drawing conclusions and analyzing results.

B) Asking questions, making a hypothesis, testing the hypothesis, analyzing the results and drawing conclusions.

C) Making a hypothesis, testing the hypothesis, analyzing the results, asking a question and drawing conclusions.

D) Asking a question, analyzing results, making a hypothesis, testing the hypothesis and drawing conclusions.

CONTINUE ▶

Coriolis effect is an effect whereby a mass moving in a rotating system experiences a force acting perpendicular to the direction of motion and to the axis of rotation.

What happens to the wind currents as influenced by the Coriolis effect?

A) The wind currents tend to cool off as they converge and rise

B) The wind flows in a straight path as it crosses lines of longitude

C) The wind currents diverge and sink, and eventually heat up

D) The wind currents tend to curve as they flow over Earth's surface

Which of the following activities is the best example of the practice of science as an inquiry?

A) Determining which objects float upon placing different objects in a tank of water.

B) Identifying the materials needed to build a terrarium.

C) Determining how long a trip will take by assessing the road conditions.

D) Following directions in constructing an electric motor.

28

Upwelling is an oceanographic phenomenon in which deep, cold water rises toward the surface.

What is the primary reason of the upwelling of cold water in the large sections of the west coasts of North and South America?

A) Due to prevailing wind patterns, water moves away from the coast.

B) The steep offshore topography that forces deep water currents upward.

C) Solar heating that caused rapid evaporation of surface water.

D) The respiration of microorganisms that caused the reduction in density of deep-ocean water.

29

The oxygen in our atmosphere is essential for life. The atmosphere blocks some of the Sun's dangerous rays from reaching Earth and makes Earth livable. It traps heat, making Earth a comfortable temperature.

Which of the following statements is not true about the atmosphere?

A) It is the layer in which weather occurs.

B) It is the layer that contains the ozone layer.

C) It is the layer of gases that surrounds the Earth.

D) It is the layer of water in the oceans.

30

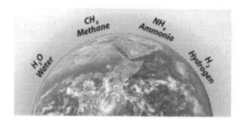

For decades, scientists believed that the atmosphere of early Earth was highly reduced.

Which of the following gas does not make up the primitive atmosphere?

A) Hydrogen

B) Ammonia

C) Oxygen

D) Water vapour

CONTINUE ▶

31

Which of the following would be the best way of confirming the suspicion of a scientist who suspects that a random error may have occurred in the data collected for his experiment?

A) Attempt to identify any factors that could have caused the random result and repeat the experiment a large number of additional times to check if the data remains consistent.

B) Recalibrate the measurement instrument and perform the experiment one additional time.

C) Have several colleagues with expertise in the field of study review his results to check for careless errors.

D) Formulate a new hypothesis and begin the experimental process again adhering to the steps of the scientific method.

32

Which of the following wave components is necessary to determine the distance of the earthquake from the station where primary and secondary seismic waves arrived?

A) Wavelengths

B) Arrival times

C) Frequencies

D) Horizontal or vertical displacements

33

What kind of device would an astronomer use in order to determine the composition of a newly discovered star?

A) A device that can determine the direction and velocity of an object.

B) A device that can analyze the frequency of absorbed or emitted light.

C) A device that can calculate the half-life of radioactive elements

D) A device that can magnify an image through a system of multiple lenses.

Which of the following is characterized by the stage depicted in the above diagram where a genetic material is attached to spindle fibers followed by nuclear membrane breakdown?

A) The assortment of chromosomes to form haploid cells in meiosis

B) The separation of sister chromatids in mitosis

C) Crossing over during mitosis

D) Nondisjunction of at least one pair of sister chromatids during meiosis

A dead tree decays.

The top of a hill erodes slowly.

A star uses up its nuclear fuel over years.

A bottle of cologne is opened and the molecules spread throughout the room.

Which of the following scientific principles is illustrated in the four phenomena described above?

A) Physical balance called equilibrium

B) A reaction to something of a response

C) A state of disorder or entropy

D) A state of total confusion with no order called chaos

In a polar covalent bond, the shared electrons are more attracted to one of the atoms than the other. The shared electrons are more likely to be near the atom whose electronegativity is higher.

Between which of the following elements the polarity of the covalent bonds would be greatest?

A) In the same column of the periodic table farthest from each other.

B) In the same row of the periodic table farthest from each other.

C) In the same row of the periodic table adjacent to each other.

D) In the same column of the periodic table adjacent to each other.

Which of the following procedures would enable a soil scientist to adequately determine the volume of the air spaces in a soil sample in a metal container?

A) Comparison of volumes between the soil sample and a rock sample of the equal mass

B) Measuring the volume of water needed to saturate the soil sample.

C) Calculating the volume of the soil sample when it is spread out in a thin layer.

D) Observing the change in volume of the soil sample as it is compacted with a heavy object

38

The body fluids in saltwater fish are lower in salinity than their salty marine habitat. It allows them to counteract the osmotic pressure exerted by the minerals dissolved in the water.

Which of the following is prevented by these fluids?

A) Loss of too many minerals from the tissues

B) Loss of too much water from the tissues

C) Absorption of too much water into the tissues

D) Absorption of too many minerals into the tissues

39

In the role of general public's support and appreciation of science, which of the following plays the most significant role?

A) Politicians who understand the value of expensive research projects that may have limited short-term benefits.

B) A business community aiming to improve competitiveness through funded research.

C) Schools providing topic and issues related to the sciences to students for broad understanding.

D) A university promoting the integration of pure research and applications of technology.

40

Which of the following information is provided by the hypothesis during a scientific investigation?

A) A question that can be answered by researching existing literature

B) A format for outlining the approach to be used in the investigation

C) A summary of previous research on the topic being investigated

D) A proposed explanation for the phenomena being investigated

41

Which of the following strategies resulted in a biased interpretation of the findings of a scientific investigation?

A) Reviewing an abstract of the data analysis before submitting an article for publication in a journal.

B) Due to known procedural errors, flawed data collected during an extensive research project were rejected.

C) A scientist, lacking modern technological resources, formulates a hypothesis based on data collected.

D) Questioning the conclusions of the research due to the failure of including experimental data.

42

According to an Arabic scholar Avicenna, mountains could only be formed over long periods of time. He supported his hypothesis with his firsthand knowledge based on several observations of geologic processes such as water erosion and the localized uplift caused by earthquakes.

Which geologic principle fundamental to modern geology did Avicenna employ to understand geologic past?

A) The original horizontality principle
B) The superposition principle
C) The cross-cutting relationships principle
D) The uniformitarianism principle

43

Human activities are partly responsible for changes in global temperatures experienced during the past 100 years.

Which of the following best explains why average global temperatures over the last 100 years is so high?

A) Natural systems do not generally shift that quickly unless disturbed by some external mechanism.
B) Natural systems are always changing, but generally at an almost constant rate.
C) Natural systems usually show randomly fluctuating rates of change over time.
D) Natural systems usually show decreasing rates of change as the system matures.

Reactants	Observation
P and Q	Turns red after three hours
Q and R	No change
P and R	No change
P, Q and R	Turns red after two minutes

The reactants P, Q, and R given above are colorless liquids. Which of the following explanation is correct?

A) In the reaction of P and Q, R acts as a catalyst.

B) The combined product of Q and R reacts with P.

C) The combined product of P and Q reacts with R.

D) In the reaction between Q and R, P acts as a catalyst.

SECTION 1

#	Answer	Topic	Subtopic	#	Answer	Topic	Subtopic	#	Answer	Topic	Subtopic	#	Answer	Topic	Subtopic
1	C	TB	SB2	12	D	TB	SB1	23	A	TA	SA3	34	B	TA	SA3
2	A	TB	SB1	13	C	TA	SA1	24	D	TA	SA1	35	C	TB	SB2
3	D	TB	SB1	14	A	TB	SB2	25	B	TA	SA1	36	B	TA	SA2
4	C	TA	SA2	15	A	TB	SB1	26	D	TB	SB1	37	B	TA	SA1
5	C	TB	SB2	16	B	TB	SB1	27	A	TA	SA1	38	B	TA	SA3
6	A	TA	SA2	17	D	TB	SB1	28	A	TB	SB1	39	C	TA	SA1
7	B	TA	SA1	18	B	TA	SA2	29	D	TB	SB1	40	D	TA	SA1
8	A	TA	SA1	19	A	TB	SB1	30	C	TB	SB1	41	D	TA	SA1
9	C	TB	SB1	20	C	TB	SB2	31	A	TA	SA1	42	D	TB	SB1
10	B	TB	SB1	21	A	TA	SA1	32	B	TA	SA2	43	A	TA	SA1
11	A	TB	SB1	22	D	TB	SB1	33	B	TB	SB2	44	A	TA	SA2

Topics & Subtopics

Code	Description	Code	Description
SA1	Nature of Science	SB2	Astronomy
SA2	Physical Science	TA	General Science
SA3	Life Science	TB	Earth & Space Science
SB1	Geology & Atmosphere		

CONTINUE ▶

TEST DIRECTION

DIRECTIONS

Read the questions carefully and then choose the ONE best answer to each question.

Be sure to allocate your time carefully so you are able to complete the entire test within the testing session. You may go back and review your answers at any time.

You may use any available space in your test booklet for scratch work.

Questions in this booklet are not actual test questions but they are the samples for commonly asked questions.

This test aims to cover all topics which may appear on the actual test. However some topics may not be covered.

Studying this booklet will be preparing you for the actual test. It will not guarantee improving your test score but it will help you pass your exam on the first attempt.

Some useful tips for answering multiple choice questions;

- Start with the questions that you can easily answer.

- Underline the keywords in the question.

- Be sure to read all the choices given.

- Watch for keywords such as NOT, always, only, all, never, completely.

- Do not forget to answer every question.

1

Dr. Moore and his colleagues are analyzing the physical factors associated with the propagation of tsunamis.

Which of the following methods would be most useful and appropriate to use by Dr. Moore's team in conducting the study?

A) Examining the patterns produced when other types of waves are disrupted.

B) Creating underwater explosions using depth charges, and recording the waves produced in each explosion.

C) Producing waves under a wide range of different conditions using a large tank in the laboratory.

D) Examining how sea wells were formed using the historical records of large earthquakes.

2

Before using a pH meter in measuring the pH of a water sample, what must a scientist do to ensure that the reading is accurate?

A) Warm the pH meter

B) Calibrate first the meter with a buffer solution.

C) Filter the sample to remove any organic matter.

D) Place the sample in a sealed container and refrigerate it.

3

The Brazilian Current in the Southern Hemisphere moves toward the South Pole, while the Gulf Stream in the Northern Hemisphere moves toward the North Pole.

What effect will this pole-ward movement bring to the coastal areas bordering these currents when compared to the inland areas at the same latitude?

A) The coastal areas will be warmer than the inland areas.

B) The coastal areas will be more arid than the inland areas.

C) The coastal areas will have more advection fogs than the inland areas.

D) The coastal areas will have shorter growing seasons than the inland areas.

4

Mr. Gregor is collecting data on the orientation of a limestone layer exposed along a highway to investigate the geologic history of a region.

What information should Mr. Gregor include in reporting the orientation of the limestone layer?

A) The depth at which the limestone was excavated

B) The angle at which the limestone was found

C) The degree of measurements showing the strike and dip of the bedding plane of the limestone

D) The changes in the dimensions of the limestone

CONTINUE ▶

5

What does a hypothesis provide in a scientific investigation?

A) A scientific question that can be answered through existing literature

B) A summary of prior studies related to the investigation topic

C) An outline of the approach to be used in the investigation

D) A proposed explanation for the phenomena being studied

6

Which of the following statements is true regarding temperature and pressure when you go deeper beneath the Earth's surface?

A) Both temperature and pressure increase

B) Both temperature and pressure decrease

C) Both temperature and pressure stay the same

D) Both temperature and pressure approach zero

7

Air is the mixture of gases that forms the Earth's atmosphere and that we breathe.

Which of the following is the major gas in the air?

A) Oxygen

B) Nitrogen

C) Hydrogen

D) Carbon dioxide

8

Which of the following is a correct explanation about rocks and minerals?

A) Minerals are classified by their chemical composition and physical properties, while rocks are classified by their formation and the minerals they contain.

B) Traces of organic compounds may be found in minerals but not in rocks.

C) Mineraloids are both contained by rocks and minerals.

D) Minerals and rocks are both polymorphs.

9

Which element comprises the most significant amount of rocks and minerals?

A) Carbon (C)
B) Aluminum (Al)
C) Hydrogen (H)
D) Silicon (Si)

11

Plant cell

Which of the following describes the distinct function of the central vacuole in plant cells?

A) It maintains hydrostatic pressure.
B) It strengthens the cell.
C) It stores energy-rich compounds produced in the cell.
D) It controls the movement of substances into and out of the cell.

10

What makes mathematics be considered as the language of science?

A) Mathematics and science rely on the same processes.
B) Mathematics describes testable and predictable relationships.
C) Mathematics reduces the uncertainties of chaotic systems.
D) Mathematics has no cultural biases.

12

A fundamental concept of the cell theory is best summarized by which of the following statements?

A) Each cell has its own DNA and RNA.
B) Living organisms are composed of one or more cells.
C) To maintain health, living organisms rely on specialized cells.
D) Cells break down of molecules to produce energy.

CONTINUE ▶

A pond has become choked with weeds. To determine the actual dissolved oxygen content of the pond, a hydrologist is collecting water samples.

Which sample collection method should the hydrologist use to most closely reflect the actual dissolved oxygen content of the pond water?

A) Collecting water samples from below the pond's surface in various locations, filling and then sealing the containers rapidly and recording the locations.

B) Collecting water samples from the pond's surface near the outlet where the water is moving rapidly, and few weeds are growing.

C) Collecting the water sample from near the pond's inlet and avoid including any organisms or debris that may be in the water.

D) Collecting the water sample from near the bottom, making sure to leave some air space in the container and including some of the organic matter found in the pond.

What type of bond is responsible for water tension and the formation of water drops?

A) Covalent bond

B) Ionic bond

C) Nuclear bond

D) Hydrogen bond

Dr. Hover collects and tests the pH of water from six local ponds after significant rainstorms to determine whether rainfall increases the acidity of pond water.

What makes Dr. Hover's experiment design unreliable?

A) It does not have a clear hypothesis.
B) It has no manipulated variables.
C) It has no control data.
D) It has no dependent variables.

By volume, dry air contains 78.09% nitrogen, 0.93% argon, 0.04% carbon dioxide, and small amounts of other gases. Air also contains a variable amount of water vapor, on average around 1% at sea level, and 0.4% over the entire atmosphere.

What is the average concentration of oxygen in the ambient air?

A) 10.95%
B) 20.95%
C) 25.95%
D) 30.95%

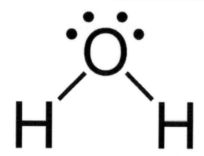

Which of the following explains why water is capable of mechanical weathering?

A) It has a high surface tension

B) It has a very high capacity to store heat energy

C) It increases in density as it goes from 0 °C to 4°C and then decreases above 4°C

D) It increases in volume as it goes from a liquid to a solid state

What is the primary effect of Coriolis force on ocean surface currents?

A) It causes the currents to curve from a straight path.

B) It causes the currents to expand as they enter cool waters.

C) It increases the friction between currents and ocean floor.

D) It decreases the speed of the currents relative to adjacent ocean waters or land masses.

19

Weathering is the breaking down of rocks, soil, and minerals as well as wood and artificial materials by the action of rainwater, extremes of temperature, and biological activity. There are three types of weathering, physical (mechanical), chemical and biological.

How does mechanical weathering differ from chemical weathering?

A) Mechanical weathering leaves the composition of the rock unchanged.

B) Mechanical weathering causes decomposition of rock through organic acids.

C) Mechanical weathering breaks down rock through hydrolysis.

D) Mechanical weathering changes rock through the process of oxidation.

20

Which of the following is the description of loudness in an acoustic wave?

A) The rate of vibrations

B) The period of wavelengths

C) The magnitude of pressure variations

D) The number of cycles per second

21

According to statistical evaluation, the global temperatures experienced during the past 100 years is higher than at any time during the past 1,000 years.

Which explanation supports a claim that human activities over the last 100 years are partly responsible for this increase?

A) Any shifts in natural systems do not happen quickly unless perturbed by some external mechanisms like human activities.

B) As the system matures, it's normal for it to show decreasing rates of change.

C) Changes in natural systems happen at an almost constant rate.

D) Changes in natural systems happen at fluctuating rates.

22

Why does the sky appear blue?

A) Because the air molecules selectively scatter the shorter wavelengths of visible light

B) Because the air molecules reflect the longer wavelengths of visible light

C) Because the water vapor refracts visible light into its component frequencies

D) Because the water vapor selectively absorbs visible light at particular wavelengths

CONTINUE ▶

23

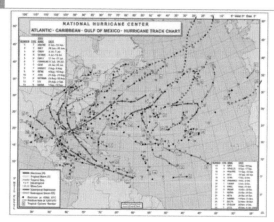

Which phenomenon primarily causes the formation of Atlantic hurricanes between June and November?

A) The subtropical jet stream's position during these months

B) An increased activity of the northeast trade winds during these months

C) The average sea surface temperature in the Atlantic during these months

D) The northward shift of the inter-tropical convergence zone during these months

24

Which of the following geologic events caused the formation of the Atlantic Ocean?

A) The erosion of a plate margin caused by repeated continental glaciations

B) The subduction of one continental plate beneath another

C) The development of a large syncline east of the Appalachian Mountains

D) The growth of a rift valley along a primary fracture zone in the crust

25

What is the primary reason why lunar eclipses occur much less frequently than the days moon orbits Earth?

A) The plane of the moon's orbit around Earth is tilted relative to the plane of Earth's orbit around the sun.

B) The tilt of Earth's axis relative to the sun changes regularly as Earth orbits the sun.

C) The distance from Earth to the sun is greater than the distance from Earth to the moon.

D) The speed of Earth's orbit around the sun is greater than the moon's orbital speed around Earth.

26

Climate is defined as the weather conditions that are characteristic of an area in general or over a long period.

What are the two main factors that determine the climate of a region?

A) Temperature and precipitation

B) Pressure and temperature

C) Altitude and pressure

D) Altitude and temperature

CONTINUE ▶

27

Scientists believe that up to 99% of all species of organisms that ever lived on Earth are now extinct as well as the belief that humans will never know anything about many of these species because there are no fossils of them in the Earth's fossil record.

Which of the following statements best explains the reason why this is true?

I. Most species had bodies that were too small to undergo fossilization.

II. Fossils of most extinct organisms have been converted to fossil fuels by geologic processes.

III. Many species did not possess hard body parts that would fossilize readily.

IV. Many species did not live in environments in which fossilization was likely to occur.

A) I and II
B) I and IV
C) II and III
D) III and IV

28

Which of the following is a correct explanation about rocks and minerals?

A) Minerals are classified by their chemical composition and physical properties, while rocks are classified by their formation and the minerals they contain.
B) Traces of organic compounds may be found in minerals but not in rocks.
C) Mineraloids are both contained by rocks and minerals.
D) Minerals and rocks are both polymorphs.

According to the scientists, which of the following is the source of the Earth's magnetic field?

A) The Earth's core has a current of charged particles moving around it

B) The Earth's orbit passes through a stream of charged particles emitted by the sun

C) The Earth's mantle and crust consist of iron-rich magma with charged particles

D) The Earth's core is a large chunk of charged particles

A galaxy is a gravitationally bound system of stars, stellar remnants, interstellar gasses, dust, and dark matter. Recent estimates made by astronomers say that there are more than a billion galaxies in the observable universe and they are usually categorized based on their shape.

Which of the following shape is taken by our galaxy, the Milky Way?

A) Spiral Galaxy

B) Cloud Galaxy

C) Elliptical Galaxy

D) Irregular Galaxy

31

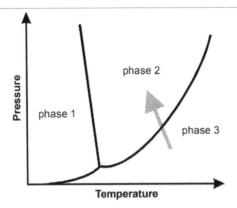

In the water phase-change above, which of the following processes is represented by the gray arrow?

A) Evaporation or the change from liquid to gas

B) Melting or the change from solid to liquid

C) Freezing or the change from liquid to solid

D) Condensation or the change from gas to liquid

32

Greenhouse Gases in the atmosphere absorbs and emits radiation within the thermal infrared range. Some of the Greenhouse Gases are water vapor, carbon dioxide, nitrous oxide, etc.

Which of the following is also a greenhouse gas?

A) Propane

B) Methane

C) Helium

D) Butane

33

A metamorphic rock is a type of rock which has been changed by extreme heat and pressure. Its name is from 'meta' (meaning change), and 'morph' (meaning form).

Gerold is a meteorologist and he wants to find out if the rock samples collected are metamorphic.

Which of the following is a property of a metamorphic rock?

A) It has tiny holes and spaces.
B) It has interlocking minerals with some foliation.
C) It has straight or wavy stripes of different colors.
D) It has a shiny, smooth surface but without a crystalline structure.

34

Upon gas expansion, which of the following phenomena is characterized by the inverse relationship between temperature and density?

A) Water vapor evaporation during hot days
B) Water vapor condensation during cool nights
C) Convection currents during warm days
D) Water vapor sublimation during cool dry days

35

The **water cycle** describes how water evaporates from the surface of the earth, rises into the atmosphere, cools and condenses into rain or snow in clouds, and falls again to the surface as precipitation.

Which of the following terms is not associated with the water cycle?

A) Precipitation
B) Transpiration
C) Evaporation
D) Fixation

36

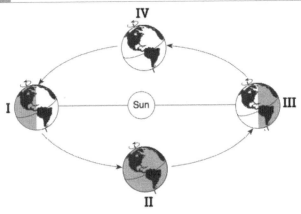

The figure above shows Earth orbiting the Sun while it is rotating about its axis once every 24 hours.

Which change in seasons occurs in the Northern Hemisphere at position IV?

A) Winter is ending, and spring is beginning.

B) Spring is ending, and summer is beginning.

C) Summer is ending, and fall is beginning.

D) Fall is ending, and winter is beginning.

37

What is the basis for the acceptance of James Watson and Francis Crick's three-dimensional model of the DNA molecule?

A) Its ability to explain the mechanism of DNA replication and its integration with existing evidence on genetics.

B) The collected data, before their research was begun, about the use of the DNA molecule.

C) Analysis of the DNA molecule through the use of state-of-the-art technology.

D) Its ability to explain the roles of the enzyme in DNA transcription and the quality of the researcher's published work.

38

Which of the following information is provided by the hypothesis during a scientific investigation?

A) A question that can be answered by researching existing literature

B) A format for outlining the approach to be used in the investigation

C) A summary of previous research on the topic being investigated

D) A proposed explanation for the phenomena being investigated

39

What must scientists do to isolate the relationship between two variables in an experiment?

A) Experiment with a laboratory setting

B) Predict the full range of possible outcomes of the experiment

C) Control the conditions under which the experiment is carried out

D) Limit the scope of the experiment to the investigation of known facts

40

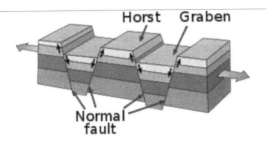

Horst   Graben

Normal
fault

In geology, horst and graben refer to regions that lie between normal faults and are either higher or lower than the area beyond the faults.

The formation of the horst and graben structures of the Basin and Range Province of the western United States was a result of which of the following?

A) The differential erosion of sedimentary rocks and volcanic rocks for the past million years

B) The tensional forces that caused the occurrence of crustal extension of the North American Plate

C) The erosion and deposition cycles associated with the multiple glaciations during the Pleistocene period

D) The compressional forces that caused the uplift of the North American Plate

41

An energy change that occurs as water evaporates from a pond on a warm day is best described by which of the following?

A) Water molecules move into the lower energy state due to the lower average kinetic energy of air compared to water.

B) The average kinetic energy of the water reduces as faster-moving water molecules break free from the water's surface.

C) Decreased in the average kinetic energy of the overlying air due to the adsorption of slower-moving water molecules on the surface.

D) Increased in the total kinetic energy of the air due to air molecules that pull water molecules into the gaseous phase.

Apollo MX is a space shuttle that is orbiting the Earth. It fires its rocket engine to adjust its course eventually.

Which of the following is the mechanism that allows the shuttle to change its course?

A) Pressure behind the shuttle is being increased by the emitted heat energy coming from the engines to move the spacecraft forward.

B) The thin air below the shuttle is being pushed by the hot gases of the engines to propel the spacecraft.

C) Air molecules are being pulled into the engines via combustion to push the spacecraft forward.

D) There is an equal and opposite force exerted by the hot gases and the spacecraft.

The reason why astronomical telescopes designed to receive radio signals often have larger surface areas than optical telescopes is best explained by which of the following statements?

A) Radio waves have greater interference from Earth-based sources than visible light.

B) Visible light has more energy and higher frequency than radio waves.

C) Radio waves do not travel in straight lines while light does.

D) As they pass through Earth's atmosphere, radio waves are refracted less than visible light.

Among the following events, which one would be least likely to occur at a significantly smaller scale?

A) Sediment is formed into a stream due to the erosion of a hillside.

B) A star is formed from an interstellar dust cloud due to gravitational attraction.

C) The discharge of static electricity produces a lightning bolt during a storm.

D) The electric currents in the Earth's outer core generate a magnetic field.

SECTION 2

#	Answer	Topic	Subtopic	#	Answer	Topic	Subtopic	#	Answer	Topic	Subtopic	#	Answer	Topic	Subtopic
1	C	TA	SA1	12	B	TA	SA3	23	C	TB	SB1	34	C	TA	SA2
2	B	TA	SA1	13	A	TA	SA1	24	D	TB	SB1	35	D	TA	SA2
3	A	TB	SB1	14	D	TA	SA2	25	A	TB	SB2	36	D	TB	SB2
4	C	TA	SA1	15	C	TA	SA1	26	A	TB	SB1	37	A	TA	SA3
5	D	TA	SA1	16	B	TB	SB1	27	D	TA	SA3	38	D	TA	SA1
6	A	TB	SB1	17	D	TA	SA2	28	B	TB	SB1	39	C	TA	SA1
7	B	TB	SB1	18	A	TB	SB1	29	A	TB	SB1	40	B	TB	SB1
8	A	TB	SB1	19	A	TB	SB1	30	A	TB	SB2	41	B	TA	SA2
9	A	TB	SB1	20	C	TA	SA2	31	D	TA	SA2	42	D	TA	SA3
10	B	TA	SA1	21	A	TA	SA1	32	B	TB	SB1	43	B	TB	SB2
11	A	TA	SA3	22	A	TB	SB1	33	B	TB	SB1	44	B	TB	SB1

Topics & Subtopics

Code	Description	Code	Description
SA1	Nature of Science	SB2	Astronomy
SA2	Physical Science	TA	General Science
SA3	Life Science	TB	Earth & Space Science
SB1	Geology & Atmosphere		

CONTINUE ▶

TEST DIRECTION

DIRECTIONS

Read the questions carefully and then choose the ONE best answer to each question.

Be sure to allocate your time carefully so you are able to complete the entire test within the testing session. You may go back and review your answers at any time.

You may use any available space in your test booklet for scratch work.

Questions in this booklet are not actual test questions but they are the samples for commonly asked questions.

This test aims to cover all topics which may appear on the actual test. However some topics may not be covered.

Studying this booklet will be preparing you for the actual test. It will not guarantee improving your test score but it will help you pass your exam on the first attempt.

Some useful tips for answering multiple choice questions;

- Start with the questions that you can easily answer.

- Underline the keywords in the question.

- Be sure to read all the choices given.

- Watch for keywords such as NOT, always, only, all, never, completely.

- Do not forget to answer every question.

Due to which of the following an enormous amount of energy is released in an atomic explosion?

A) The result of the conversion of chemical energy into nuclear energy

B) The result of the conversions of neutrons into protons

C) The result of the conversion of mechanical energy into nuclear energy

D) The result of the conversion of mass into energy

The USGS installs seismographs near a dormant volcano to detect the increases in tremors that might indicate a coming eruption.

What other actions would be most useful in providing information for predicting an eruption of the volcano?

A) Surveying the vicinity of the volcano for a possible development of sinkholes.

B) Detecting any possible slight changes in elevation of the land surrounding the volcano through installing tiltmeters.

C) Keeping a record of the daily variations in the humidity of the air in the vicinity of the volcano.

D) Detecting any possible increase in acidity through monitoring the pH level of rainfall in the area.

3

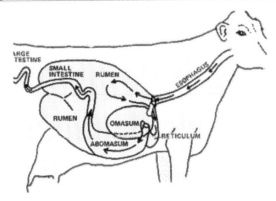

What is the primary function of dividing the digestive systems of ruminant animals into several different chambers?

A) To extract and meet daily water needs

B) To synthesize the required proteins from simple carbohydrates

C) To allow continuous feed of animal before digestion

D) To use microbial action to break down and extract nutrients from hard-to-digest substances such as cellulose

4

Which of the following has provided the most information about the structure of Earth's core, mantle, and lower crust?

A) Analysis of Active Lava Flows

B) Collection of samples from deep boreholes drilled into Earth

C) Measurement of the intensity and fluctuations of Earth's magnetic field

D) Studies of the speeds and travel paths of seismic waves passing through Earth

5

Why do overcast nights tend to be warmer than clear nights even when temperatures on a preceding day have been the same?

A) Because on overcast nights, the evaporation rates are substantially reduced

B) Because the clouds radiate infrared energy downward during overcast nights

C) Because the convection currents are unable to develop during overcast nights

D) Because on overcast nights, water vapor condenses and releases energy

6

Air contains essential substances, such as oxygen and nitrogen. These gases make up about 99 percent of Earth's atmosphere. People need oxygen to live. Carbon dioxide, a gas that plants depend on, makes up less than .04 percent.

What is the approximate percentage of oxygen in the air at sea level?

A) 5%

B) 10%

C) 15%

D) 20%

7

Which of the following is the element present in the largest amount of rocks and minerals?

A) Carbon

B) Magnesium

C) Silicon

D) Hydrogen

8

Which of the following will the scientist need, in addition to a balance and a ruler, to determine the magnitude of the unbalanced force acting on an object as it falls?

A) Digital timer

B) Steel protactor

C) Spring scale

D) 100mL graduated cylinder

9

In a closed electric circuit, which of the following copper wires has the smallest resistance?

A) Long wire with a large diameter

B) Long wire with a small diameter

C) Short wire with a large diameter

D) Short wire with a small diameter

10

The collision between a continental lithospheric plate and an oceanic lithospheric plate can lead to the formation of which of the following?

A) A mid-oceanic ridge

B) A chain of coastal volcanic mountains

C) Arc a transform fault

D) A volcanic island

11

The Atlantic Ocean began to form as a result of which of the following geologic events?

A) The erosion of a plate margin from repeated continental glaciations

B) The subduction of one continental plate beneath another

C) The development of a large syncline east of the Appalachian Mountains

D) The growth of a rift valley along a major fracture zone in the crust

CONTINUE ▶

12

In predicting whether the skies will change from clear to cloudy, which of the following would give the most useful information?

A) Relative humidity
B) Temperature
C) Barometric pressure
D) Wind speed

13

What causes the colorful displays in the atmosphere called the aurora borealis?

A) The nuclear disintegration of radioactive isotopes in the thermosphere
B) The combustion of dust particles in the stratosphere
C) The chemical reaction of molecules in the troposphere
D) The interaction of the solar wind and the magnetosphere, causing excitation of gases

14

A controlled experiment is a scientific test that is directly manipulated by a scientist.

Which of the following is a controlled experiment designed for?

A) Data
B) Hypothesis
C) Conclusion
D) Measurement

15

Which of the following does an element's atomic number tell?

A) The number of electrons
B) The number of protons
C) Total number of protons and neutrons
D) Total number of electrons and protons

16

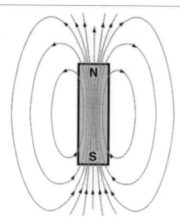

A bar magnet was placed at the bottom of a paper. The iron filings that were previously scattered onto the paper, became aligned along the magnetic field lines similar to that of the image above.

Which of the following causes this behavior of iron filings?

A) The magnetic field of the earth attracts the fillings

B) The fillings are magnetized by the magnetic field

C) The filings are repelled by the induced electric field

D) The magnetic field ionizes the fillings

17

What was the primary cause of the changes to the Earth's climate system, causing the 1991 eruption of Mount Pinatubo in the Philippines?

A) The accumulation of sulfur dioxide in the lower stratosphere

B) The accumulation of some particulates that were trapped in the upper troposphere

C) The accumulation of carbon dioxide in the upper stratosphere

D) The accumulation of nitrogen oxide that increased smog in the lower troposphere

18

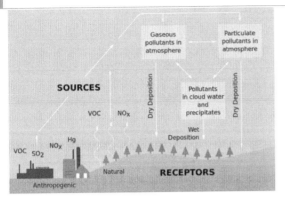

Which of the following can effectively reduce acid precipitation from power plant emissions?

A) Using lime and water in exhausts to react sulfur dioxide with calcium hydroxide

B) Using mesh filtration systems to filter dust particles generated by the breakdown of coal

C) Using smokestack catalytic converters to convert carbon monoxide to carbon dioxide

D) Removing volatile hydrocarbon compounds found in coal before burning the fuel

19

Mr. Fleming collects temperature data for the past 50 years from the Midwest. The data show a steady increase in daytime summer temperatures.

How can Mr. Fleming use these data to make predictions about how the average temperatures may increase in the following years?

A) Make a graphical presentation of the data, showing the line of best fit into the coming years.

B) Calculate the range of the data set and assume any future increases will be within that range.

C) Calculate the probable temperature for the coming year by adding the median of the data set and the average calculated temperature for each coming year.

D) Calculate the total change over time in the data set and use it in determining the minimum increase in the future.

20

If an unbalanced force acts on an object, then the object will begin to accelerate.

Which of the following law explains this situation?

A) Kepler's Laws of Motion
B) Newton's First Law
C) Newton's Second Law
D) Newton's Third Law

21

A particulate matter (PM), also known as particle pollution, is an atmospheric pollutant. What comprises a particulate matter?

A) Gases and acidic liquids
B) Small fragments of natural substances visible to the unaided eye
C) Solid materials and droplets which are small enough to be suspended in the air
D) Chemicals that trap heat and absorb infrared energy

22

The temperature of the air nearest the ground surface often drops as sunlight strikes damp ground shortly after sunrise.

Which of the following best explains this early morning cooling of the air?

A) The condensation of water from water vapor
B) The sublimation of water vapor from the ground surface
C) The phase change of water from liquid to gas
D) The sensible heat decreases as the humidity near the ground surface increases

23

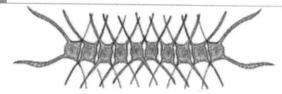

Phytoplanktons are single-celled organisms which are similar to terrestrial plants in that they contain chlorophyll and require sunlight in order to live and grow.

How does a phytoplankton help in balancing the Earth's climate?

A) It takes in ozone and produces diatomic oxygen.
B) It absorbs carbon dioxide and produces oxygen.
C) It uses nitrogen oxides and produces methane.
D) It takes in water vapor and produces carbon dioxide.

CONTINUE ▶

Which of the following shows how a physical model can be used to understand a complex natural system?

A) Dr. Murphy examines the rocks containing fossils to reconstruct the habitat of an extinct fossilized animal.

B) Dr. Lewis predicts winter weather for the next several years using historical data correlating sunspot cycles with short-term temperature changes.

C) Dr. Carter locates a deposit of oil and natural gases by measuring changes in the speed and direction of seismic waves produced by explosions or earthquakes.

D) Dr. Wenger made a scaled-down replica of San Francisco Bay to assess how a tsunami might affect the region.

Which of the following important consequences for the soil in desert and grassland ecosystems is caused by an irrigation used over a long period of time?

A) Natural soil micro-organisms were depleted

B) Upper soil horizons accumulate salts

C) Erosion and consequent loss of topsoil

D) Fungal pathogens below the soil surface increases

26

Which of the following is the primary factor responsible for the variability in average annual temperatures in Arizona?

A) The range in elevation in different parts of the stat

B) The extreme changes in wind direction that occur over the course of the year

C) The extent of the rain shadows that exist on the leeward sides of some mountains

D) The intense radiational cooling that occurs in some locations in the state

27

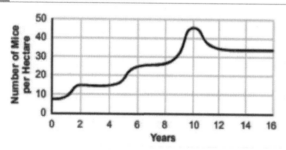

Based on the graph above that illustrates change over time in a population of nonnative mice in a forest, what is the approximate number of the ecosystem's carrying capacity for the mouse population?

A) 15 mice per hectare.

B) 25 mice per hectare.

C) 35 mice per hectare.

D) 45 mice per hectare.

28

Which of the following is the independent variable in an experiment which measures the growth of bacteria at different temperatures?

A) Intensity of light

B) Temperature

C) The growth of the number of colonies

D) Type of the bacteria used

29

Abiotic factor is a nonliving condition or thing, as climate or habitat, which influences or affects an ecosystem and the organisms in it. Abiotic factors can determine which species of organisms will survive in a given environment.

Which of the following is not an abiotic factor?

A) Rainfall

B) Soil quality

C) Temperature

D) Bacteria

30

Which of the following can be further studied using a handful of information about the cycad fossils found in Arizona during the Triassic Chinle formation?

A) The relationship between the fossils and the pollinators

B) The age of the fossils

C) The location of the North American tectonic plate during that era

D) That region's ancient environment

31

The Earth is made up of different layers, and each layer has its characteristics and boundaries.

Starting from the surface of the Earth, what is the correct order of the Earth's layers?

A) The crust, outer core, inner core, mantle

B) Mantle, outer core, inner core, crust

C) Crust, mantle, outer core, the inner core

D) Outer core, inner core, crust, mantle

32

Which of the following shows the correct order of the layers of Earth's atmosphere from Earth to space?

A) Troposphere, stratosphere, mesosphere, thermosphere

B) Stratosphere, troposphere, mesosphere, thermosphere

C) Mesosphere, troposphere, stratosphere, thermosphere

D) Thermosphere, troposphere, stratosphere, mesosphere

33

Which of the following theories explain the formation of the moon?

A) A large object struck Earth, and material from both bodies combined.

B) Gravitational forces attracted materials from outer space.

C) Meteoroids collected and solidified within the pull of Earth's gravity.

D) Gases from Earth escaped from the atmosphere and condensed.

34

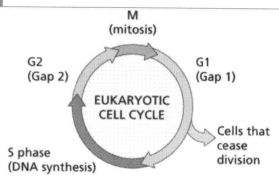

Which of the following describes how gene replication occurs in a eukaryotic cell before the cell division?

A) An amino acid is attached to a new strand of DNA by a DNA polymerase.

B) Two separate strands of DNA are added with nucleotide base pairs.

C) Complementary pairs are formed by strands of mRNA transcribed from DNA.

D) During the early phase of meiosis, chromosomes are separated into two strands of RNA.

35

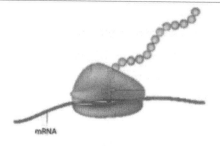

Ribonucleic acid (RNA) occurs in different forms within organisms. It serves many different roles. There are different types of RNA

In animal cells, which of the following is the primary role of the messenger RNA (mRNA)?

A) To serve as a template for the manufacture of new DNA strands within the cell nucleus.

B) To deliver amino acids to the ribosome.

C) To transfer the information needed from DNA to the ribosome.

D) To store long-term information.

36

The idea of continental drift, developed by Alfred Wegener in 1912, has been subsumed by the theory of plate tectonics, which explains how the continents move.

Which of the following pieces of evidence was used by Alfred Wegener to validate his Theory of Continental Drift?

A) Larger fault lines due to earthquakes

B) Two plant fossils from different continents were similar

C) Continental margins have mountain buildings

D) The frequent eruption of volcanoes around the Pacific Ocean

37

Many of the mountaintops in the Sierra Nevada mountain range are exposed granitic batholiths that have eroded into rounded domes, known as exfoliation domes.

What process could have led to the formation of these exfoliation domes?

A) The sheeting of substantial concentric slabs due to the unloading of pressure

B) The chemical weathering of potassium ions found in the surface of rocks

C) The erosion of granite during high runoff periods

D) The fluctuation of temperatures causing the rock face to shrink and swell

38

Which of the following is the most important thing a teacher do to maintain a safe learning environment for the laboratory activity which covers pH determination?

A) Ensure that there are no electrical devices in the working areas

B) Make a list of students who are responsible enough to handle the chemicals

C) Review procedures for handling the chemicals being investigated

D) Review the reactions that occur between the chemicals being investigated

39

Which of the following elements is present in the largest amount of rocks and minerals?

A) Carbon

B) Silicon

C) Hydrogen

D) Aluminum

40

A researcher is investigating the geologic history of a region. Which of the following information would typically be included in the data he collects on the orientation of a limestone layer exposed along a highway?

A) The thickness of the limestone and how it has changed from its original horizontal position

B) The angle between an imaginary vertical line and the uppermost surface of the limestone

C) The degree measurements that show the strike and dip of the bedding plane of the limestone

D) The meters below the land surface of different sections of the top of the exposed part of the limestone

41

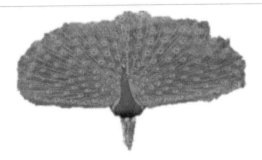

Which of the following facts can explain the evolutionary development in the sexual characteristics of male species of ground birds which make them attracted to mates and predators?

A) Predators can be drawn away better with brightly colored males.

B) The development of these sexual characteristics is accompanied by a heightened awareness of nearby predator.

C) Once the development of sexual differences between males and females has begun, reversing is hard.

D) For a long-term survival, the successful attraction of mates is more important than the longevity of individual males.

42

The intrusive igneous rocks that are composed of unusually large crystals are called pegmatites.

Which condition can typically result in the formation of pegmatites?

A) The solidification of magma bodies below the extinct volcanoes

B) The crystallization of rocks at slow rates and the high temperatures near the boundary between the mantle and the crust

C) The solidification of the granitic batholiths, leaving fluid-rich residual melt

D) The crystallization at relatively fast rates as magma flows rapidly away from its source to form a sill

CONTINUE ▶

43

A team of scientists sets up multiple strainmeters on either side of an active strike-slip fault to determine the deformation of the bedrock before minor earthquakes. This data is then correlated with seismograms for the same area. Both data sets were collected over a 20-year time frame, which will help the scientists determine if there are patterns in the deformation data that consistently precede minor earthquakes on the fault observed.

Given the information on the experiment, which of the following factors is the dependent variable?

A) The movement of the land surface during minor earthquakes

B) The types of seismic waves generated during minor earthquakes

C) The deformation of the bedrock prior to minor earthquakes

D) The frequency of fault activity resulting in minor earthquakes

44

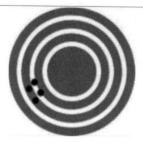

Which of the following will most directly affect the precision of the data the chemist collects in weighing the products of a chemical reaction?

A) The choice of weighing equipment to be used

B) The zeroing step on the scale before weighing

C) Establishing an average weight for the products through the use of repeated trials

D) The products' molecular weight reliance on accepted standard values

SECTION 3

#	Answer	Topic	Subtopic	#	Answer	Topic	Subtopic	#	Answer	Topic	Subtopic	#	Answer	Topic	Subtopic
1	D	TA	SA2	12	C	TB	SB1	23	B	TB	SB1	34	B	TA	SA3
2	B	TA	SA1	13	D	TB	SB1	24	D	TA	SA1	35	C	TA	SA3
3	D	TA	SA3	14	B	TA	SA1	25	B	TB	SB1	36	B	TB	SB1
4	D	TB	SB1	15	B	TA	SA2	26	A	TB	SB1	37	A	TB	SB1
5	B	TB	SB1	16	B	TA	SA2	27	C	TA	SA3	38	C	TA	SA1
6	D	TB	SB1	17	A	TB	SB1	28	B	TA	SA1	39	A	TB	SB1
7	A	TA	SA2	18	A	TB	SB1	29	D	TA	SA3	40	C	TA	SA1
8	A	TA	SA2	19	A	TA	SA1	30	D	TB	SB1	41	D	TA	SA3
9	C	TA	SA2	20	C	TA	SA2	31	C	TB	SB1	42	C	TB	SB1
10	B	TB	SB1	21	C	TB	SB1	32	A	TB	SB1	43	C	TA	SA1
11	D	TB	SB1	22	C	TB	SB1	33	A	TB	SB2	44	A	TA	SA1

Topics & Subtopics

Code	Description	Code	Description
SA1	Nature of Science	SB2	Astronomy
SA2	Physical Science	TA	General Science
SA3	Life Science	TB	Earth & Space Science
SB1	Geology & Atmosphere		

CONTINUE ▶

TEST DIRECTION

Read the questions carefully and then choose the ONE best answer to each question.

Be sure to allocate your time carefully so you are able to complete the entire test within the testing session. You may go back and review your answers at any time.

You may use any available space in your test booklet for scratch work.

Questions in this booklet are not actual test questions but they are the samples for commonly asked questions.

This test aims to cover all topics which may appear on the actual test. However some topics may not be covered.

Studying this booklet will be preparing you for the actual test. It will not guarantee improving your test score but it will help you pass your exam on the first attempt.

Some useful tips for answering multiple choice questions;

- Start with the questions that you can easily answer.

- Underline the keywords in the question.

- Be sure to read all the choices given.

- Watch for keywords such as NOT, always, only, all, never, completely.

- Do not forget to answer every question.

1

An organism that attempts to maintain homeostasis is best illustrated by which of the following examples?

A) Animal looking for a place to hibernate for the winter

B) Each year's return of migratory bird to its nesting place

C) Lowering of internal body temperature when a human sweats on a hot day

D) A butterfly larva eats plants that make it toxic to predators

2

The Earth atmosphere is composed of many gases that are vital for the survival of all living organisms.

Which of the following pairs of gases lists the two most abundant gases in the Earth's atmosphere?

A) Carbon dioxide and oxygen

B) Carbon dioxide and nitrogen

C) Nitrogen and oxygen

D) Nitrogen and hydrogen

3

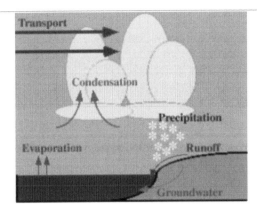

In the hydrologic cycle, water molecules absorb energy during which of the following process?

A) During the formation of ice from water

B) In the formation of a cloud from water vapor

C) The runoff along the land surface

D) The evaporation above the surface of the ocean

4

What generally happens when a warm air mass and a colder air mass converge at Earth's surface?

A) The sky becomes clear.

B) Wind movement drastically stops.

C) The clouds form slowly.

D) Stormy weather patterns develop.

5

Computer models are used to investigate possible consequences of increased average global temperatures on various Earth systems.

Based on these models, which change is likely to occur in the Earth's systems that are mostly associated with an increase in average global temperatures?

A) There will be long periods without adequate rainfall, resulting in some regions' experiencing drier droughts.

B) There will be rapid changes in weather conditions as a result of an increased frequency of jet stream winds' position shifting.

C) Coriolis effect will be stronger, causing a reduced occurrence of hurricanes in tropical areas.

D) Anomalous weather conditions such as El Niño will occur at longer intervals.

6

Which of the following condition must be present for a low-pressure system to continue to develop into a stronger low-pressure system?

A) The divergent wind flow occurring at the base of the low-pressure system

B) The cold-air advection occurring above the low- pressure system

C) The convection of relatively warm air within the low-pressure system

D) The convergent wind flow occurring above the low-pressure system

7

What causes the air moving from the poles toward the equator to turn westward?

A) The size and shape of land masses near the path of the wind

B) The larger cities surrounded by farmlands

C) The sudden changes in the magnetic field of the Earth

D) The rotation of the Earth

8

Alfred Wegener was the first to propose the theory of continental drift in which he explained that continents had changed position over time. However, many scientists rejected his approach despite having some compelling evidence of his claim.

What was the primary scientific reason causing many geologists to reject Wegener's continental drift proposal?

A) He was considered an amateur who was trained in a different scientific discipline.

B) His hypothesis lacked a convincing mechanism to explain what forces moved the continents.

C) He believed his evidence was strong; hence he did not argue the merits of his ideas.

D) His fieldwork lacked the rigor associated with most sciences of the day.

9

The presence of a layer of conglomerate in bedrock just above a layer of shale is consistent with the sequences of events involving which of the following?

A) Cooling and hardening of lava over a layer of rock from a volcanic eruption

B) Lowering the water level of a large lake, which eventually formed into a beach

C) Accumulation of shells developed from one-celled organisms

D) Localized recrystallization of shale from mud deposits

10

In which areas of Earth and space science research does the analysis of the ratio of the oxygen isotopes O-18 and O-16 play an essential role?

A) In calculating the age of lavas from the volcanic eruptions during the Pleistocene era

B) In determining the global temperature relative changes during the Quaternary period

C) In determining the carbon dioxide concentration in gas bubbles of some sheets of ice

D) In finding the rates at which sedimentation occurs on the abyssal plains in ocean deeps

11

This landform is an area of highland that has a relatively flat terrain at its surface. It is elevated significantly compared to its surroundings and is also known by other names such as high plain or tableland.

Which of the following is another name given to landform?

A) Lowland

B) Mountain System

C) Coastal Plain

D) Plateau

CONTINUE ▶

Which of the following measures would be least likely affected by the limitation in the recording equipment which records air temperature higher than 100°F as being equal to 100°F?

A) Mode
B) Median
C) Range
D) Mean

A scientific team collects data on twenty lakes in different regions of the US to study acid rain. A rain gauge is placed at each lake, and the amount and pH of precipitation that falls each week is recorded. At the same time, the scientists measure the pH of each lake's water and the slope of the ground within 100 meters of each lake's shore.

What is the dependent variable of this study?

A) The measured slope of the ground around each lake
B) The precipitation pH level
C) The amount of precipitation
D) The pH level of each lake's water

CONTINUE ▶

14

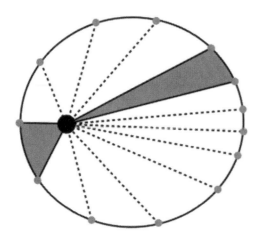

Which of the following is not one of Kepler's Laws of Planetary Motion?

A) All planets move about the Sun in elliptical orbits, having the Sun as one of the foci.

B) Planets move on elliptical orbits with the Sun at one focus.

C) An imaginary line drawn from the center of the sun to the center of the planet will sweep out equal areas in equal intervals of time.

D) The ratio of the squares of the periods of any two planets is equal to the ratio of the cubes of their average distances from the sun.

15

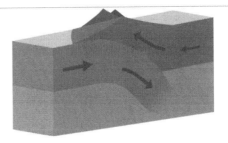

When two tectonic plates of different densities converge, which of the following features is formed?

A) A transform fault

B) An oceanic ridge

C) A transform fault

D) A deep-sea trench

16

Onshore and offshore winds occur over the areas where land masses meet large bodies of water.

Which of the following is the reason why onshore and offshore winds occur?

A) Water has a higher specific heat than land

B) The land has a higher specific heat than water

C) The land absorbs more thermal energy

D) Water cannot absorb as much thermal energy as the land

17

What must a scientist do to isolate the relationship between two variables in an experiment?

A) Make sure to experiment in a laboratory

B) Identify the scope of the investigation

C) Make sure to control the conditions that can alter the experiment

D) Make predictions of the full range of the experiment's possible outcomes

18

Which of the following about the scientists is not correct?

A) Galileo Galilei is best known for describing the laws of planetary motion.

B) Sir Charles Lyell is best known for uniformitarianism, the idea that geological change is a prolonged process.

C) Edwin Hubble was an American astronomer who, in 1925, was the first to demonstrate the existence of other galaxies besides the Milky Way.

D) Nicolaus Copernicus was a Renaissance-era mathematician and astronomer who proposed the heliocentric solar system, in which the sun, rather than the earth, is the center of the solar system.

19

Which of the following organism is most responsible for fixing atmospheric carbon dioxide to create organic molecules?

A) Coral polyps

B) Bacteria

C) Phytoplankton

D) Protozoa

20

Which geologic materials cannot typically withstand shaking caused by a major earthquake?

A) Materials made up of heavily fractured shale

B) Materials made up of karstic limestone

C) The unconsolidated silt and clay materials

D) The massive granite materials

21

Freshwater accounts for approximately 3% of the water on Earth. In which area freshwater is most likely be found?

A) Groundwater

B) In the atmosphere

C) Lakes and ponds

D) Glaciers and ice caps

22

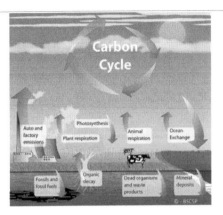

The carbon cycle occurs in the atmosphere, the hydrosphere, the biosphere, and the lithosphere.

Which of the following events describes one step in the movement of carbon from the atmosphere to the lithosphere?

A) Carbonic acid is produced from limestone during weathering.

B) Bicarbonate ions are extracted from seawater during coral reef formation.

C) Carbon dioxide is formed during the decay of biomass.

D) Atomic carbon is absorbed in seawater by deep-ocean sediments.

23

Some of the wave properties are defined below. Which of the following is not a correct explanation?

A) Wavelength is the distance between adjacent crests, measured in meters.

B) The period is the time it takes for one complete wave to pass a given point.

C) Frequency is the number of complete waves that pass a point in one second.

D) Amplitude is the height of the wave, in other words, it is the distance from the top of the crest to the bottom of the adjacent trough.

24

Which of the following can be accounted for the soil formation in mountainous regions?

A) The erosion and sediment deposition

B) The gradual movement of tectonic plates

C) The mechanical and chemical rock weathering

D) The decomposition through fungi and bacteria

25

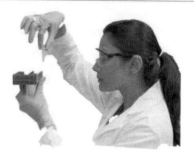

Which of the following is the most important thing a scientist should do to demonstrate to the scientific community that her discovery is legitimate?

A) Call for a press conference and announce her research.

B) Repeat the experiment in the presence of neutral observers.

C) Provide verifiable evidence to support her claim.

D) Explain the mechanism involved in her discovery.

26

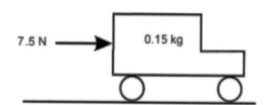

What is the acceleration of a toy truck weighing 0.15 kg as it is being pushed with a constant force of 7.5 N?

A) 0.02 m/s2

B) 50.0 m/s2

C) 5.0 m/s2

D) The toy truck's acceleration cannot be determined.

Which of the following characteristics of Venus is most directly related to the timing of its appearance at dawn and dusk?

A) Venus is one of the brightest objects in the sky.

B) Venus has a slower rotation time than any other planet in the solar system.

C) The plane of Venus's orbit is tilted relative to the plane of the orbit of Earth.

D) The orbit of Venus is between the sun and the orbit of Earth.

The percentage of cells in a sample that is in each of the five phases of replication – interphase, prophase, metaphase, anaphase, telophase – was analyzed by a biologist.

If the total of all the cells counted was 73 and 19 of the cells came from the telophase, what is the percentage of cells in the telophase?

A) 39%

B) 35%

C) 26%

D) 23%

Which of the following is the best way for a scientist to make predictions about how the average temperatures in the Midwest may increase in the following years using the temperature data collected from the same area over the past 50 years?

A) Plot the data set and extend the line of best fit into the coming years.

B) Determine the range of the data set and assume any future increases will be within that range.

C) Take the median of the dataset and add that to the average temperature for each coming year.

D) Calculate the total change over time in the data set and assume it reflects the minimum increase in the future.

## 30

Which of the following regulates the passage of ions and polar molecules in and out of a cell?

A) The attached carbohydrates to the membrane's outer surface.

B) The opening and closing of vacuoles adjacent to the membrane.

C) A selectively permeable cell membrane's phospholipid bilayer.

D) The diffusion gradient between the inside and outside of the membrane.

31

Which of the following statements best describe the chemical makeup of a saltwater solution?

A) Uniform distribution of individual sodium and chloride ions among water molecules

B) Water molecules surrounding clusters of sodium and chloride crystals

C) Water molecules surrounding clusters of sodium chloride molecules

D) Uniform distribution of individual molecules of sodium chloride among the water molecules

32

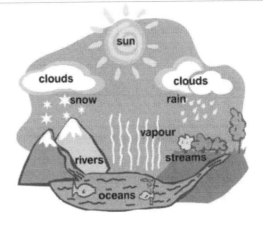

The water cycle is the cycle of processes by which water circulates between the earth's oceans, atmosphere, and land, involving precipitation as rain and snow, drainage in streams and rivers, and return to the atmosphere by evaporation and transpiration.

What is true of the water cycle?

A) Some part of the water is groundwater.

B) Two percent of the water is fixed and unavailable.

C) The ocean currents drive the water cycle.

D) Surface water is unavailable if iced.

33

Tides are the rise and fall of sea levels caused by the combined effects of the gravitational forces exerted by the Moon and the Sun and the rotation of Earth.

Which of the following is the main cause of the existence of tides?

A) Water moves due to the Earth's rotation on its axis.

B) Strong winds blow water onto the coasts causing tides.

C) Tides are caused by the differences in how much the sun pulls on different parts of the Earth.

D) Tides are caused by the differences in how much the moon pulls on different parts of the Earth.

34

Which of the following questions would provide the best foundation for a climatologist who is investigating the causes of an extended drought in a particular region?

A) How long did other droughts in the region last?

B) What variables affect the region's precipitation during droughts?

C) How could the drought conditions in the region best be managed?

D) Why do droughts strike only in specific regions and not in others?

35

Which of the following are the rocks formed from previously existing rocks that have been modified by temperature, pressure, and mechanical stress?

A) Basaltic rocks

B) Igneous rocks

C) Metamorphic rocks

D) Sedimentary rocks

36

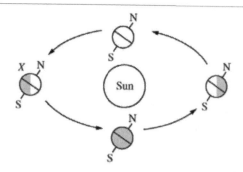

Earth's orbit around the Sun is given above. Which of the following is true of the Earth at location X?

A) The spring equinox occurs.

B) The fall equinox occurs.

C) The winter solstice occurs in the northern hemisphere.

D) The summer solstice occurs in the northern hemisphere.

CONTINUE ▶

37

A pond has become choked with weeds and a hydrologist wants to determinate the dissolved oxygen content of the pond.

Which of the following methods should the hydrologist use to effectively collect water samples so that she will be able to find the dissolved oxygen content of the pond?

A) The water should be collected from below the pond's surface in various locations, filling and then sealing the containers rapidly and recording the locations.

B) The samples should be collected from the pond's surface near the outlet where the water is moving rapidly and few weeds are growing.

C) The water should be collected from near the bottom, making sure to leave some air space in the container and including some of the organic matter found in the pond.

D) The samples should be collected near the pond's inlet and should avoid including any organisms or debris that may be in the water.

38

In the competition between organisms, which of the following is most generally true?

A) When resources are not sufficient, native species typically pish out non-native species.

B) Resource partitioning is more characteristic of animal species than of plant species.

C) There is a more intense competition between members of the same species than members of different species.

D) Competition is more likely to happen between species that occupy the same niche than species in different niches.

## 39

In which of the following areas of Earth and space research is the analysis of the ratio of the oxygen isotopes O-18 and O-16 extremely useful?

A) Calculating the age of lava flows from Pleistocene era volcanic eruptions

B) Determining relative changes in global temperature during the Quaternary period

C) Calculating the concentration of carbon dioxide in gas bubbles trapped in ice sheets

D) Determining sedimentation rates on the abyssal plains of the deep oceans

## 40

A high-yield drinking-water well draws water from a confined aquifer. A scientist wants to determine the source of the contaminant. In his investigation, he discovers that the test wells drilled to the north and east of the deep well were contaminated while the test wells drilled to the south and west were not.

The scientist then concludes that the contaminant must be coming from the north and east.

Which of the following factors would most likely reduce the validity of the scientist's conclusion?

A) The contaminated samples were collected on the same day by different people.

B) The contaminated test wells are on the upgradient side of the drinking water well where groundwater in the confined aquifer flows toward the well.

C) The uncontaminated samples were collected when the pump for the drinking water well was on, while the other samples were collected when it was off.

D) The uncontaminated test wells were drilled to a depth that is above the confined aquifer supplying water to the drinking water well.

SECTION 4

#	Answer	Topic	Subtopic	#	Answer	Topic	Subtopic	#	Answer	Topic	Subtopic	#	Answer	Topic	Subtopic
1	C	TA	SA3	11	D	TB	SB1	21	D	TB	SB1	31	A	TA	SA2
2	C	TB	SB1	12	B	TA	SA1	22	B	TA	SA2	32	B	TA	SA2
3	D	TA	SA2	13	D	TA	SA1	23	D	TA	SA2	33	D	TB	SB2
4	D	TB	SB1	14	B	TA	SA2	24	C	TB	SB1	34	B	TA	SA1
5	A	TB	SB1	15	D	TB	SB1	25	C	TA	SA1	35	C	TB	SB1
6	C	TB	SB1	16	A	TB	SB1	26	C	TA	SA2	36	A	TB	SB2
7	D	TB	SB1	17	C	TA	SA1	27	D	TB	SB2	37	A	TA	SA1
8	B	TB	SB1	18	A	TA	SA2	28	C	TA	SA3	38	D	TA	SA3
9	B	TB	SB1	19	C	TA	SA3	29	A	TA	SA1	39	B	TB	SB1
10	B	TB	SB1	20	C	TB	SB1	30	C	TA	SA3	40	D	TA	SA1

Topics & Subtopics

Code	Description	Code	Description
SA1	Nature of Science	SB2	Astronomy
SA2	Physical Science	TA	General Science
SA3	Life Science	TB	Earth & Space Science
SB1	Geology & Atmosphere		

72
CONTINUE ▶

TEST DIRECTION

Read the questions carefully and then choose the ONE best answer to each question.

Be sure to allocate your time carefully so you are able to complete the entire test within the testing session. You may go back and review your answers at any time.

You may use any available space in your test booklet for scratch work.

Questions in this booklet are not actual test questions but they are the samples for commonly asked questions.

This test aims to cover all topics which may appear on the actual test. However some topics may not be covered.

Studying this booklet will be preparing you for the actual test. It will not guarantee improving your test score but it will help you pass your exam on the first attempt.

Some useful tips for answering multiple choice questions;

- Start with the questions that you can easily answer.

- Underline the keywords in the question.

- Be sure to read all the choices given.

- Watch for keywords such as NOT, always, only, all, never, completely.

- Do not forget to answer every question.

CONTINUE ▶

1

An **ideal gas** is a theoretical gas composed of many randomly moving point particles whose only interactions are perfectly elastic collisions.

For an ideal gas when all other conditions are constant which of the following variables are inversely proportional?

A) Pressure and temperature

B) Pressure and the number of moles

C) Pressure and volume

D) No two variables are inversely proportional

2

A controlled experiment is a scientific test done under controlled conditions. Only one factor is changed at a time, while all others are kept constant.

Which of the following conclusion is true for a controlled experiment?

A) The conclusion must show that the data support the hypothesis.

B) The conclusion must show that the hypothesis was incorrect.

C) The conclusion must be reached for every experiment.

D) The conclusion must relate the data to the hypothesis.

3

If the population of bacteria in a culture flask doubles every 15 minutes, the population after 1 hour and 30 minutes will be how many times the population at the start?

A) 16

B) 32

C) 64

D) 128

4

Which of the following about the vapor pressure of the liquid is true when a liquid is at its boiling point?

A) It is greater than the external pressure on the liquid.

B) It is equal to the external pressure on the liquid.

C) It is less than the external pressure on the liquid.

D) It can be either less or greater than the external pressure on the liquid.

5

$$2KNO_3 \longrightarrow 2KNO_2 + O_2$$

How many moles of gaseous oxygen are released if six moles of potassium nitrate decomposes?

A) 5 moles

B) 4 moles

C) 3 moles

D) 2 moles

6

Which of the following is not one of Kepler's Laws of Planetary Motion?

A) The moon passes through the earth's shadow

B) The moon passes through the sun's shadow

C) Earth passes through the moon's shadow

D) Earth passes through the sun's shadow

7

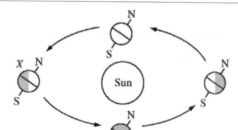

Earth's orbit around the Sun is given above. Which of the following is true of the Earth at location X?

A) The spring equinox occurs at X

B) The fall equinox occurs at X

C) The northern hemisphere experiences winter solstice

D) The northern hemisphere experiences summer solstice

8

A group of hydrologists wants to determine the average discharge of a particular river over the past 100 years using historical data.

What measure is best to use to determine the variability of this data set?

A) The median of the data set

B) The standard deviation of the dataset

C) The mode of the dataset

D) The arithmetic mean of the dataset

A chart shows the amount of rain each month in a region.

What does the expression given above mean for a scientist?

A) Variables
B) Inferences
C) Data
D) Conclusions

John wants to investigate the relationship between the effort needed to slide a given object along an inclined plane and the slope of the inclined plane.

What type of inclined planes should John use?

A) Those inclined planes that are made up of the same materials and the same length, but having different slopes.

B) Those inclined planes that have different lengths, but are made of the same material and having the same slope.

C) Those inclined planes of the same length, but having different slopes and made of different materials.

D) Those inclined planes that are made up of different materials but have the same slope and length.

11

Eutrophication is the process by which a body of water becomes enriched in dissolved nutrients (such as phosphates) that stimulate the growth of aquatic plant life usually resulting in the depletion of dissolved oxygen.

How is it possible to conclude that eutrophication of bodies of water has occurred?

A) By testing for the level of water acidity

B) By having greater species diversity in the water massive algae blooms

C) By having a vibrant, productive aquatic ecosystem

D) By having massive algae blooms

12

Which of the following chemical processes generates the energy required for metabolic activities for most organisms?

A) Breaking down of glucose molecules

B) Breaking down of protein molecules

C) Synthesis of Glycogen molecules

D) Synthesis of Lipid molecules

13

A passive margin is a transition between oceanic and continental lithosphere that is not an active plate margin.

Which of the following geologic structures characterizes a passive continental margin?

A) A thick sedimentary platform on or beneath the Earth's surface

B) An inundated forearc basin in the ocean

C) A complex accretionary wedge on the Earth's surface

D) An active fault zone beneath the Earth's surface

CONTINUE ▶

Some marine habitats are identified as hypoxic dead zones. One of the first of these zones was the Chesapeake Bay of the United States.

What is the major factor in the development of this hypoxic dead zone?

A) The runoff of nutrient-rich water into the bay
B) The acidification of bay waters from an increased concentration of dissolved carbon dioxide
C) The warming of bay waters caused by the increase in average global temperatures
D) The accumulation in bay sediments of heavy metals

Diamond is a solid form of carbon with a diamond cubic crystal structure. Because of which of the following is the diamond harder than graphite?

A) Its electron configuration is different
B) Its crystalline structure is different
C) It has a tetrahedral structure
D) None of these

CONTINUE ▶

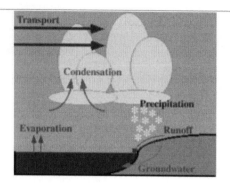

In the hydrologic cycle, water molecules absorb energy during which of the following process?

A) During the formation of ice from water

B) In the formation of a cloud from water vapor

C) The runoff along the land surface

D) The evaporation above the surface of the ocean

A researcher is analyzing a data collected for studying climate change.

In what way will the analysis become bias?

A) When the researcher notes the flaws in the research design that may have produced faulty data.

B) When the researcher removes data that significantly differ from expected results.

C) When the researcher alters the graphical presentation of the data set to make it clearer.

D) When the researcher summarizes the daily data in a weekly average.

18

Multiple strainmeters were set up on either side of an active strike-slip fault to determine how the bedrock deforms before minor earthquakes. The collected deformation data was correlated with seismograms for the area from the same period to help the scientists to learn if there are patterns in the deformation data that consistently precede minor earthquakes on the fault.

Which of the following is the dependent variable in the experiment given above?

A) Land surface's movement caused by minor earthquakes

B) Different seismic waves observed in minor earthquakes

C) Bedrock deformation before minor earthquakes

D) The intensity of the minor earthquakes for every fault activity

19

Which of the questions below would provide the best foundation for a climatologist's investigation of the causes of an extended drought in a region?

A) Why do droughts strike only in certain regions?

B) What variables affect the amount of precipitation received in the region during droughts?

C) How long is the average occurrence of droughts in other regions?

D) How could we manage the drought conditions in the region be best prevented?

20

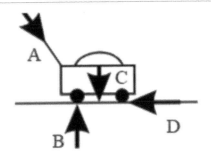

Which of the following vectors in the diagram represents the normal force?

A) A

B) B

C) C

D) D

21

Which of the following steps is critical to do before using a pH meter to determine the pH of a water sample to ensure that the reading will be accurate?

A) The sample should be refrigerated in a sealed container.

B) The meter should be calibrated with a buffer solution.

C) The meter should be allowed to warm up.

D) The sample should be filtered to remove any organic matter.

CONTINUE ▶

22

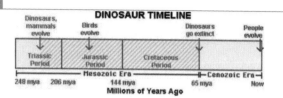

Scientists believe the rapid evolution and diversification of species that occurred at the beginning of the Mesozoic era was the consequence of which of the following?

A) The breakup of the supercontinent Pangaea in the Late Paleozoic period

B) Changes in atmospheric composition resulting from the appearance of photosynthetic organisms

C) The extinction of the majority of species near the end of the Permian period

D) Changes in the rate of genetic mutations resulting from the Sun's increased output of harmful radiation

23

In which of the following situations would professional scientific journals be most likely to reject an article for publication?

A) If an explanatory theory does not accompany the results

B) When the results contradict the findings of previous investigations

C) When the article lacks information about the methods used in the study

D) If the research is not based on the analysis of quantitative data

24

A scientist wants to determine the amount of carbon-14 in a sample of organic matter. Which of the following procedure would be the best way of this investigation?

A) A biologist establishing the metabolic rate of a cat

B) A botanist calculating the age of a living perennial herb

C) A paleontologist estimating when a dinosaur fossil formed

D) An archeologist ascertaining how long ago a fire pit was used

CONTINUE ▶

25

A Doctor wants to study the effectiveness of a CPAP Machines for sleep apnea. The Doctor records data on three groups of test subjects. The first group includes people who suffer from Apnea and are given the CPAP Machine. The second group includes people who suffer from apnea and are not given the CPAP Machine. The third group includes people who do not suffer from apnea and are given the experimental CPAP Machine.

Which of the following describes the research design for this study?

A) Observational study
B) Controlled experiment
C) Sample survey
D) None of the above

26

Which of the following scientific concepts was debunked by Einstein's Theory of Relativity?

A) Bohr's atomic model
B) Law of Conservation of Matter
C) Duality of Nature
D) Law of Inertia

27

Hydrologists use historical data to determine the average discharge of a particular river over the past 100 years to help establish the variability of the discharge of the river.

Which of the following is the best measure of the variability of this data set?

A) The median
B) The mode
C) The standard deviation
D) The arithmetic mean

28

In the cycle of carbon in the earth's ecosystems, carbon dioxide is fixed by photosynthetic organisms to form organic nutrients and is ultimately restored to the inorganic state by respiration, protoplasmic decay, or combustion.

Which of the following is not true of the carbon cycle?

A) Carbon dioxide (CO_2) is fixed by glycosylation
B) 10% of all available carbon (C) is in the air
C) Plants fix carbon (C) in the form of glucose
D) Animals release carbon through respiration

CONTINUE ▶

29

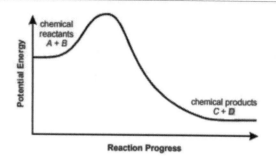

What is the indication of the higher potential energy of the reactants compared to the products?

A) As the products form, chemical energy will increase.

B) As the reactants combine, kinetic energy will decrease.

C) During the reaction, heat energy will be released.

D) During the reaction, heat energy will be absorbed.

30

Which of the following actions would most strongly bias the analysis of a researcher who is analyzing the data collected for a study of climate change?

A) Noting flaws in the research design that may have generated faulty data

B) Removing data that significantly differ from expected results

C) Altering the graphical presentation of the data set to make it more readable

D) Summarizing data collected on a daily basis into a weekly average

31

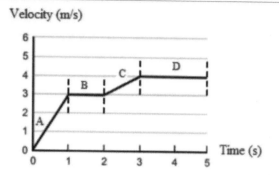

Based on the graph given above, in which time interval is the toy car's acceleration the greatest?

A) A

B) B

C) C

D) D

32

Which of the following parameter is the most common factor that limits the growth of plants in terrestrial ecosystems?

A) The soil's moisture level component

B) The level of carbon dioxide in the atmosphere

C) The level of carbonates in the soil

D) The nitrogen level in the atmosphere

CONTINUE ▶

33

In which of the following ways natural selection would most likely affect the population of zebras that lives on a savanna?

A) A considerable decrease in the mutation rate within the population.

B) A gradual decrease in the number of nonadaptive traits within the population.

C) A significant increase in the level of genetic variation within the population.

D) A substantial increase in the number of individuals in the population.

34

In biology and genealogy, the common ancestor is the ancestor that two or more descendants have in common.

Which of the following information provides with the strongest evidence that two different species share a common ancestor?

A) Similar functions of their appendages and organs

B) Their similarity in habitats and ecological niches

C) Their similar mating behaviors and rearing practices

D) The similarity in the structure of their genetic material and proteins

## 35

Which of the following statement best describes the part of a plant's root system where most cell divisions occur?

A) The region just beneath the protective cap od cells at the root tip.

B) The outermost layer of cells on the outside of root hairs.

C) The central column of cells that runs the length of the root's interior.

D) The region between the root and the stem just below the ground surface.

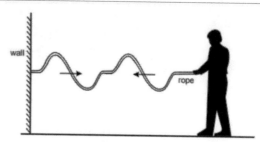

## 36

Based on the diagram given above that shows transverse wave along a rope, constructive interference of two waves will increase which of the following properties?

A) Frequency

B) Wavelength

C) Amplitude

D) Velocity

37

What form of energy is stored in a battery in which the terminals are in contact with the rotating loops of wire that can be found in a turbine that uses wind power?

A) Mechanical energy

B) Chemical energy

C) Solar energy

D) Thermal energy

38

Which of the following best explains the reason why cellphones feel warm to touch as you recharge its battery?

A) Electric current in the wirings heat up surrounding molecules.

B) Charging the battery causes the formation of high-energy chemical bonds in the cell.

C) Electrical energy converted into chemical energy causes heat formation.

D) Electric current produces heat in the form of electromagnetic radiation.

39

Which of the following is a significant consequence of the redundancy of amino acid produced by codons which are composed of different sequences of nucleotide bases?

A) A different sequence of nucleotides produced by mutations in the codon less likely to negatively affect the gene function.

B) Presence of distinct amino acids and proteins in different types of organisms.

C) When genetic material is exposed to high-energy radiation, mutation rates of codons are greatly increased.

D) Three different nucleotides can sufficiently create coded instructions for the full diversity of living organisms.

40

Which of the following is not true about decomposers?

A) Phosphorous is added back to the soil by decomposers.

B) Ammonification is the formation of ammonia or its compounds by decomposition of organic matter.

C) The Carbon accumulated in a durable organic material is recycled by decomposers.

D) Decomposers belong to the Genus Escherichia.

SECTION 5

#	Answer	Topic	Subtopic		#	Answer	Topic	Subtopic		#	Answer	Topic	Subtopic		#	Answer	Topic	Subtopic
1	C	TA	S2		11	D	TA	S1		21	B	TA	S1		31	A	TA	S2
2	D	TA	S1		12	A	TA	S3		22	C	TA	S3		32	A	TA	S3
3	C	TA	S3		13	A	TA	S3		23	C	TA	S1		33	B	TA	S3
4	B	TA	S2		14	A	TA	S3		24	D	TA	S2		34	D	TA	S3
5	C	TA	S2		15	B	TA	S2		25	B	TA	S1		35	A	TA	S3
6	A	TA	S2		16	D	TA	S2		26	B	TA	S2		36	C	TA	S2
7	A	TA	S2		17	B	TA	S1		27	D	TA	S1		37	B	TA	S2
8	D	TA	S1		18	C	TA	S1		28	A	TA	S2		38	C	TA	S2
9	C	TA	S1		19	B	TA	S1		29	C	TA	S2		39	A	TA	S3
10	A	TA	S1		20	B	TA	S2		30	B	TA	S1		40	D	TA	S3

Topics & Subtopics

Code	Description		Code	Description
SA1	Nature of Science		SA3	Life Science
SA2	Physical Science		TA	General Science

CONTINUE ▶

Made in the USA
Middletown, DE
17 February 2021